THE PRISON ALPHABET:

AN EDUCATIONAL COLORING BOOK FOR CHILDREN OF INCARCERATED PARENTS

All rights reserved. No part of this book may be used or reproduced in any manner whatsoever without the prior written permission of the publisher.

Goldest Karat Publishing
PO Box 724621
Atlanta, GA 31139
www.goldestkarat.com

For more books aimed at children of incarcerated parents, visit www.projectironkids.com.

Copyright © 2013 by Goldest Karat Publishing, LLC
Copyright © 2013 by Dr. Bahiyyah M. Muhammad and Muntaquim Muhammad

This educational coloring book belongs to:

_____

From:

_____

Message:

_____
_____
_____
_____
_____

Introduction

More than 2.7 million children in the United States have a parent in prison, and approximately 10 million have experienced parental incarceration at some point in their lives yet literature aimed at meeting their unique needs is surprisingly low.

When a parent is incarcerated it can be very difficult to explain that to a child and while many caretakers choose to hide the truth from their children, research has shown that children who were made aware of their parent's incarceration and had an opportunity to ask questions about it were less stressed and angry than children who were lied to about their parent's whereabouts.

With that in mind, this coloring book was created to serve as a conversation starter between adults who plan to talk about parental incarceration with affected children. *The Prison Alphabet* allows each letter of the alphabet to serve as a topic of discussion, an opportunity for children to ask questions, and to color. Since many children enjoy coloring, this book can be used to talk about a difficult topic in the confines of a safe place.

The motivation for this coloring book emerged from Dr. Bahiyyah M. Muhammad's recognition that children with parents in prison have many questions about what prison life is like. During her extensive interviews with children of the incarcerated, children voiced their curiosity and concern about the daily lives of their loved ones.

By using specially developed books such as *The Prison Alphabet*, we can empower children to gain a better understanding of the experience of their loved ones behind bars, show children with parents in prison that they are not alone, and provide resources for caretakers to use to create opportunities to openly discuss the child's feelings and help them cope with their parents' absence.

The Prison Alphabet is divided into two sections:

The first section is a coloring book and uses the letters of the alphabet, from A thru Z, to explain in a child-friendly manner what life is like inside a prison using terms associated with incarceration. The second section is a discussion guide to help caretakers and counselors explain parental incarceration to a young child by providing sample responses to children's commonly asked questions about life inside prison.

How to Use This Book

The Prison Alphabet contains illustrations depicting ethnically diverse characters and can therefore be used by any race or gender. Furthermore, it provides opportunities to discuss maternal, paternal and/or familial incarceration. The coloring book is primarily created to spark conversations among children of incarcerated parents, although it certainly applies to any child experiencing the incarceration of someone they know.

This coloring book and discussion guide is for adults and children alike and can be used in numerous ways, to include the following:

1. *The Prison Alphabet* is structured so that a child and an adult can read the child-friendly definitions together as a means of sparking a conversation about each word as it relates to their loved one that is behind bars. Some children may wish to color the entire book in one siting, while others may wish to color and discuss parental incarceration over a period of one month. The pace should be decided by the child and the book can be used as frequently as the child wishes.

2. *The Prison Alphabet* can be used by adults of any age who want to gain a basic understanding of what life is like behind bars. Many people who have never been behind bars or visited a prison have a very limited understanding of incarceration and can use this book to broaden their awareness.

3. *The Prison Alphabet* can also be used by an incarcerated parent, family member or friend to explain to a child what prison is like for them. To achieve this, an incarcerated person can color a page from the book and send it to a child or family member with a letter describing how the word relates to their daily experiences behind bars. Each word can be used as a discussion topic for a letter that is written to the child. The coloring book pages can then be used by the child to be framed and displayed on their bedroom wall.

Aa

ARREST

Arrest is when a police officer takes someone to jail.

Bars are used to lock the prisoner into their room called a jail cell.

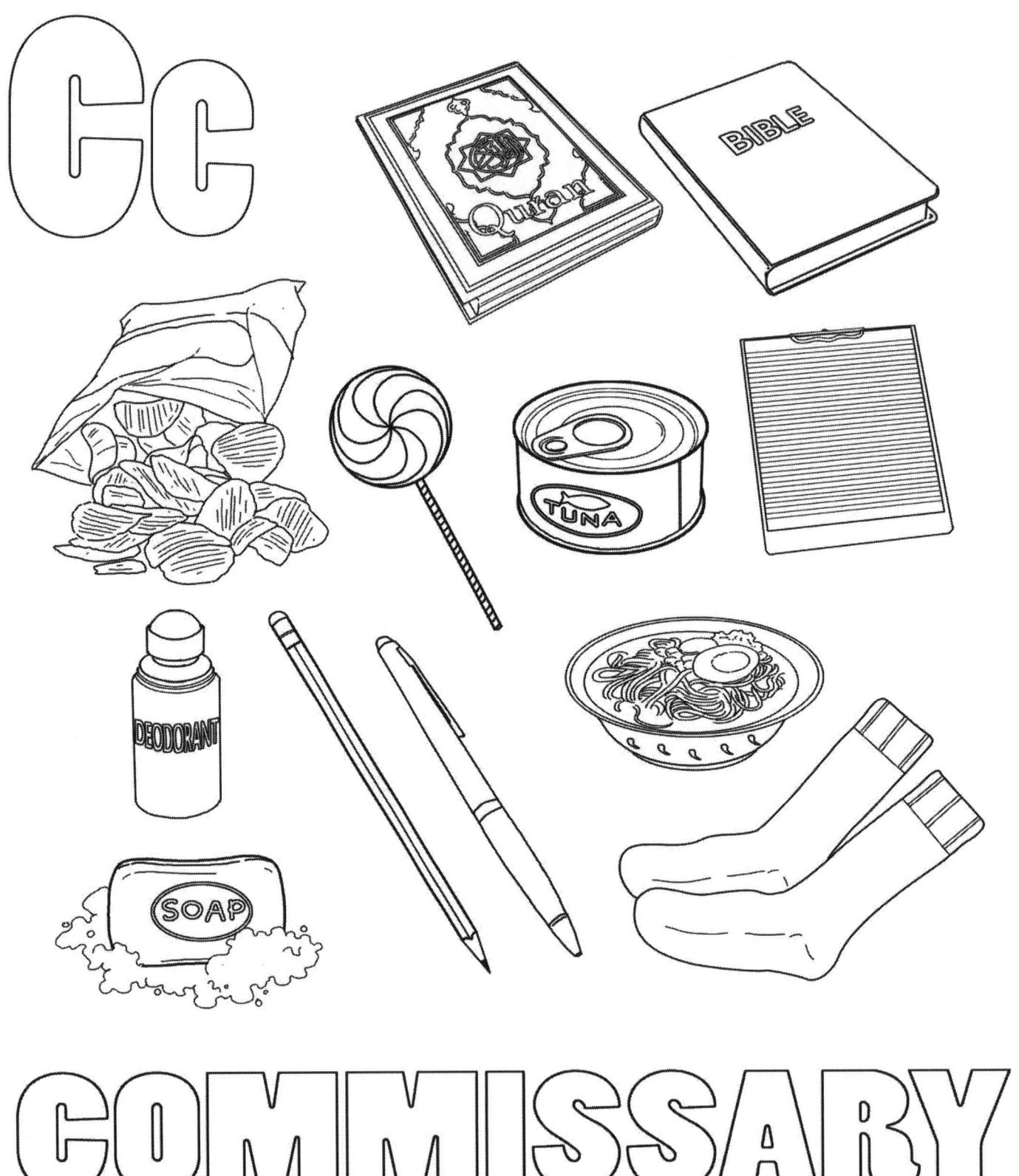

Commissary is a store inside the prison where prisoners can buy snacks, books and other items.

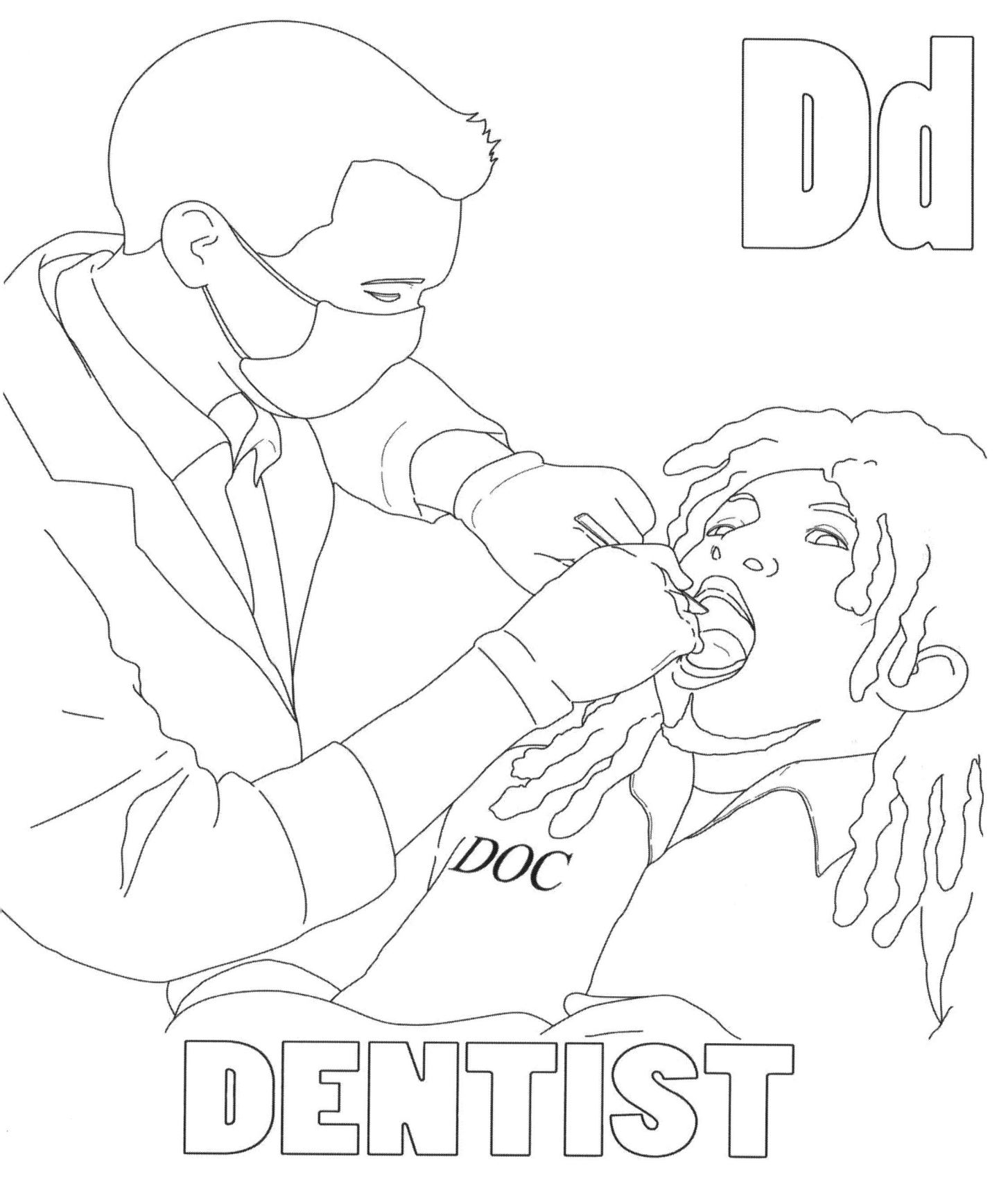

Dentists in prison make sure inmates have healthy teeth and gums. They help inmates feel better when they have toothaches.

Education means learning. Prisons have classes for inmates who want to learn.

Food is served to prisoners during breakfast, lunch and dinner.

Gg

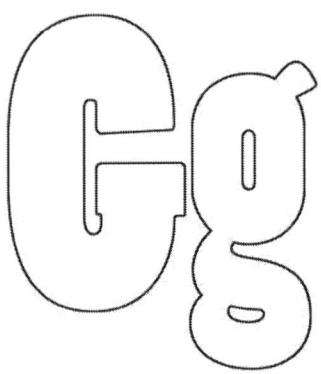

GOOD TIME

Good Time is a reward a prisoner gets for being on his or her best behavior.

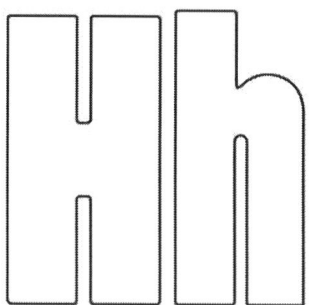

HANDCUFFS

Handcuffs are used to keep prisoners from using their hands to hurt themselves or others.

INMATES

Inmate is another word for prisoner. Inmates are people who have been sent to jail or prison because of bad behavior.

Jobs are given to prisoners to earn money while working inside the prison.

Kk

KEYS

Keys are used by guards to lock and unlock prison doors.

A **library** is a place where prisoners can go to study, read or borrow books.

Mail is delivered to the prison and given to inmates who receive letters from home.

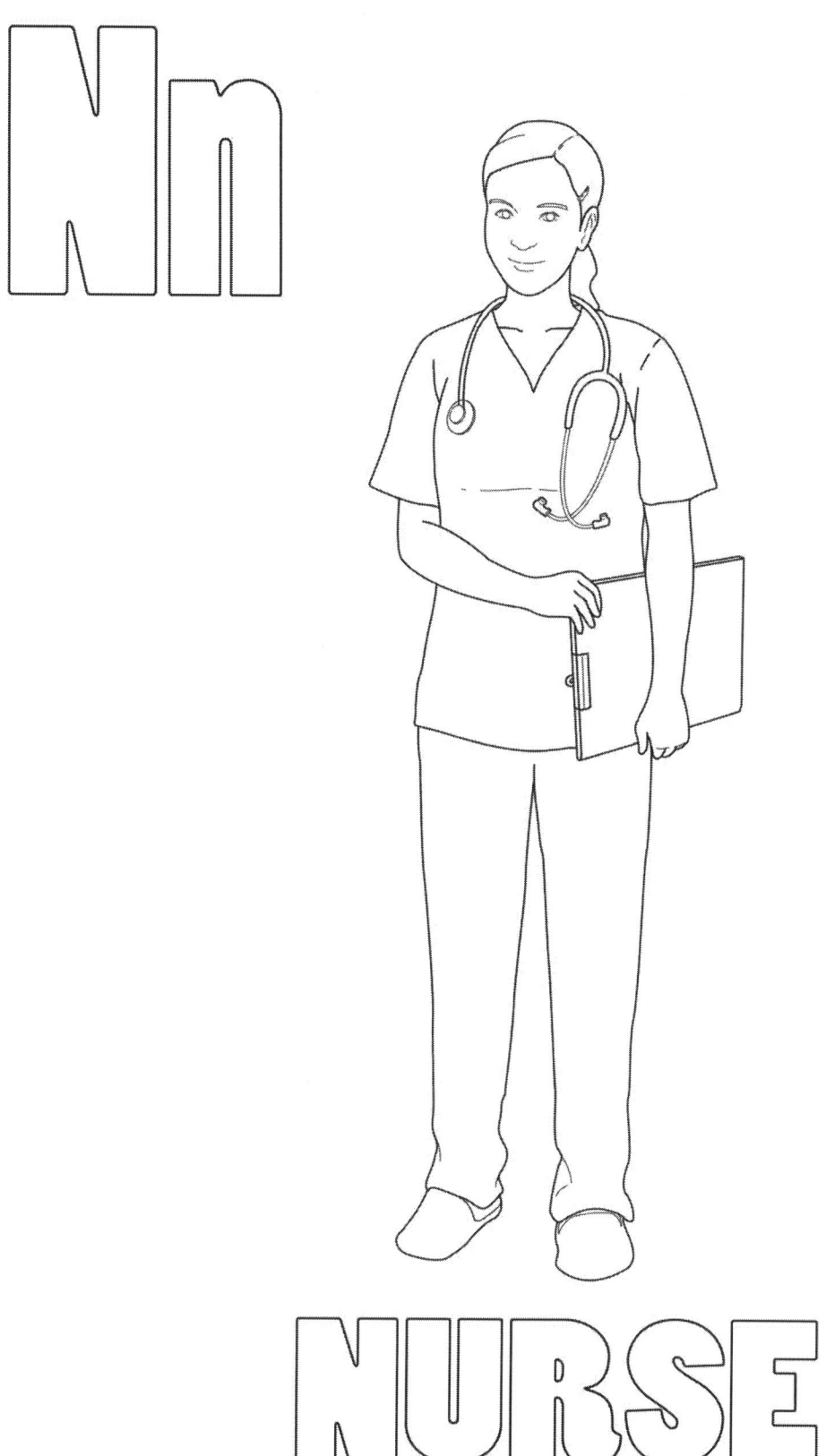

NURSE

Nurses work inside the prison and give inmates checkups when they feel sick.

OFFICER

Correctional **officers** work inside a prison or jail and monitor the everyday activities of the inmates.

Pp

PHONES

Phones are used in prison by inmates to talk with their children and loved ones.

Quiet time happens inside the prison when inmates are about to go to sleep in their beds.

Rr

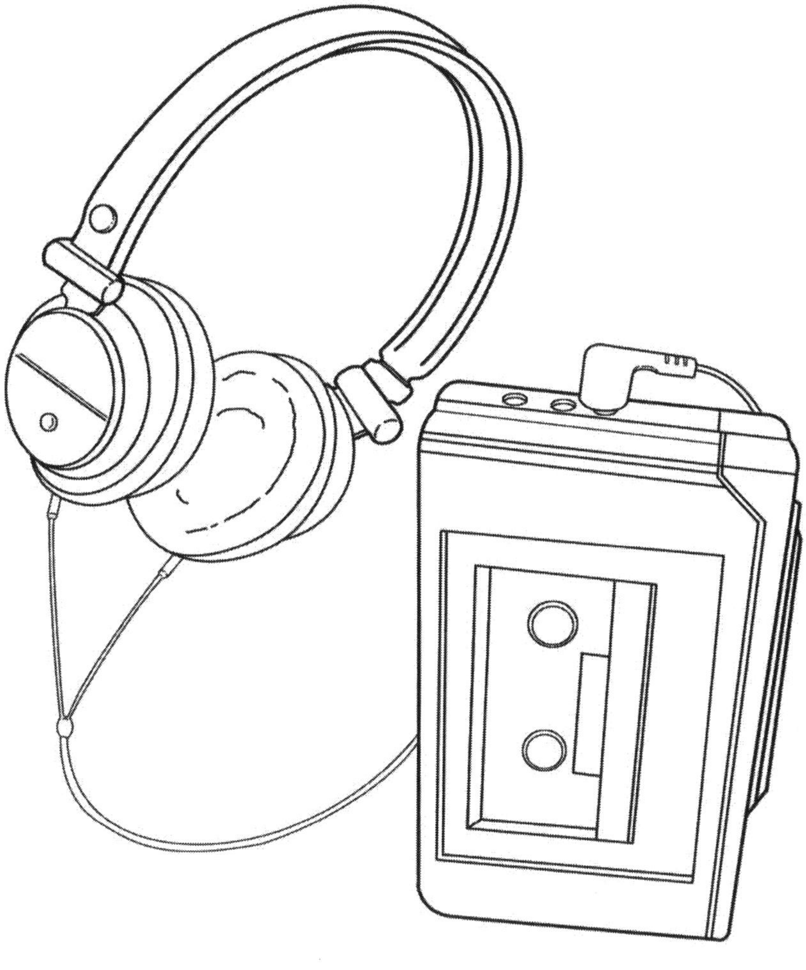

RADIO

Radios can be used in prison when inmates want to listen to their favorite songs.

Ss

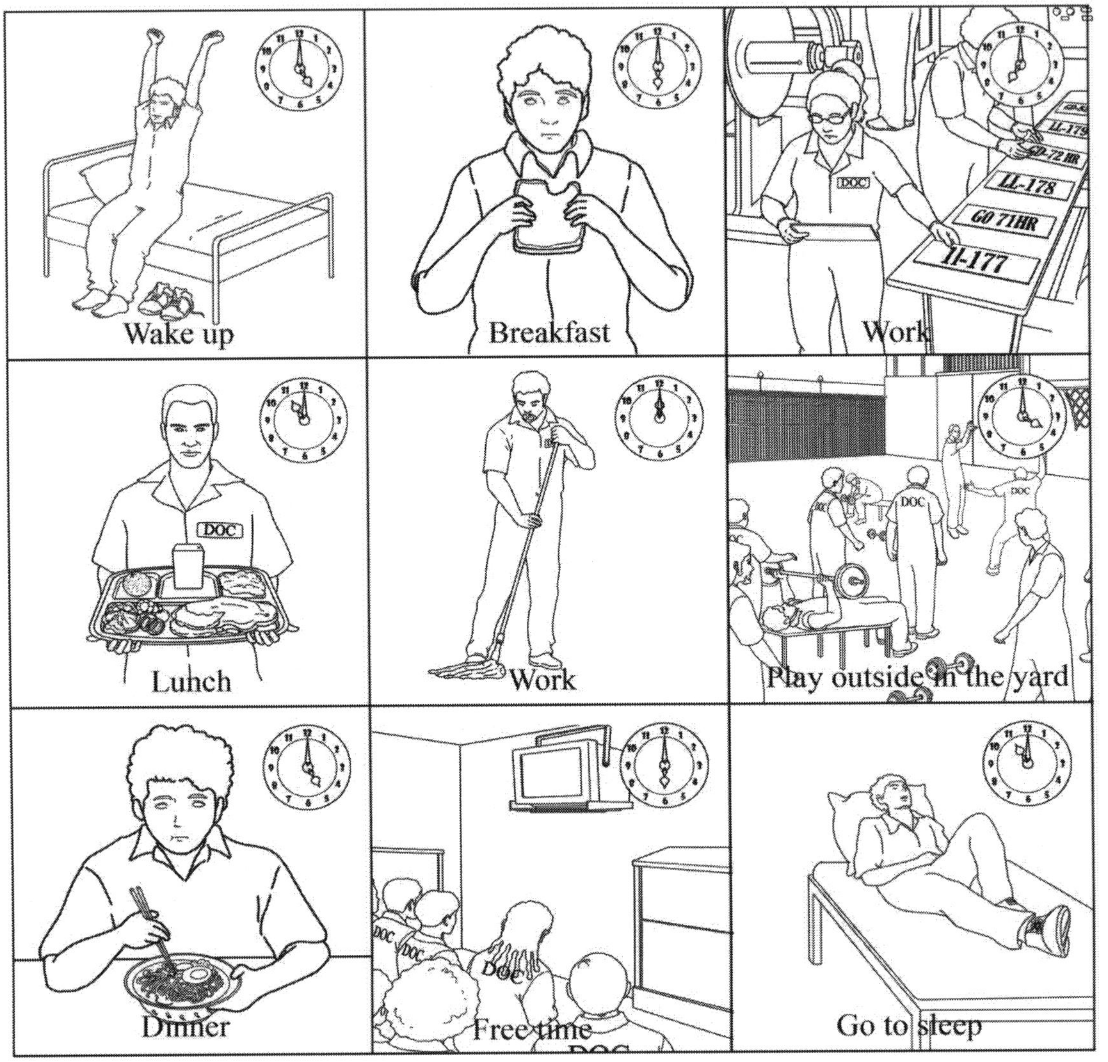

SCHEDULE

Schedules keep prisoners on time for their daily duties.

Televisions are shared by inmates who all watch TV together in a common area.

Uniforms are worn by all inmates to tell them apart from the guards.

Visits are when family and friends can go inside the prison to see their loved ones.

The **warden** is the boss of the prison and makes up all of the rules.

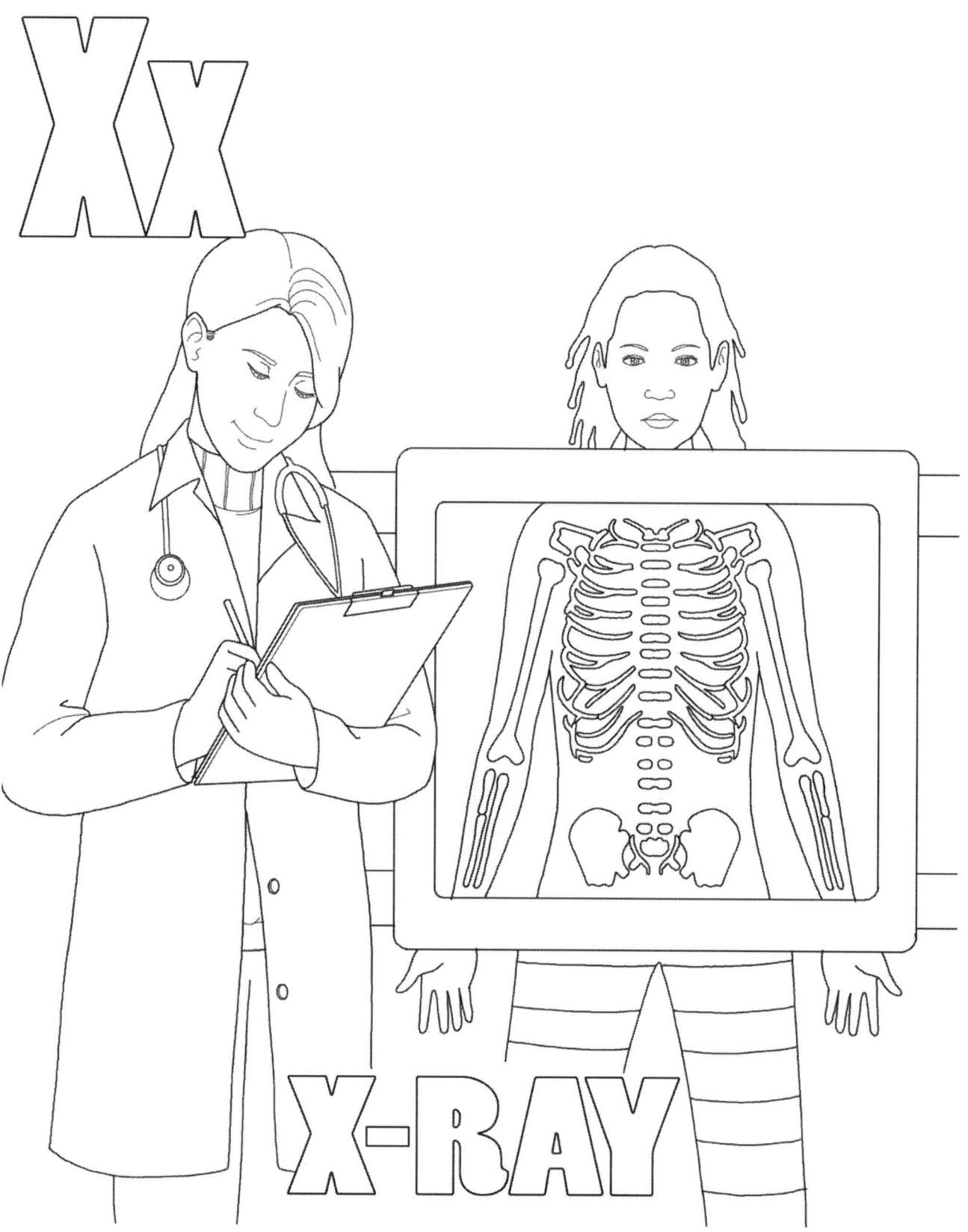

X-rays are taken by prison doctors who check inmates for broken bones.

The **yard** is an outside area where prisoners go to exercise, play sports and get fresh air.

Zoo animals are locked in cages with bars that look similar to prison cells.

Discussion Guide

The following section contains real questions that children of incarcerated parents have asked about life inside prison. For each letter of the alphabet, there is a commonly asked question along with a sample response that will help caretakers and counselors explain parental incarceration to affected children. These answers are suggestive of possible responses, not a comprehensive list of all possibilities. For more resources on how to answer difficult questions asked by children of incarcerated parents, visit www.projectironkids.com.

A is for Arrest

Is it my fault that my parent was arrested?
That is a great question. I know sometimes it feels as though you are at fault for your parent being taken away, but this is not the case. It is not your fault that your parent was arrested. Please do not blame yourself for your parent's actions.

When people are arrested it is because they have done something wrong in the eyes of the law. When an officer feels that an individual has done something against the law, they must take that individual into custody for the safety of others, including you. If a person has been found to be innocent they will be released and have permission to go home at that time.

B is for Bars

Can I sleep behind bars with my parent?
I know you miss your parent dearly, but living in prison is no place for a child. Only people who are sentenced to serve time in prison are forced to sleep there. Although you are not able to sleep behind bars with your parent, you can visit your parent during the institutions scheduled visiting days.

C is for Commissary

What kind of snacks does my parent have in prison?
That's a great question. Your parent can purchase many snacks from the prison store, which is called commissary or canteen. In the commissary you can orders snacks such as potato chips, popcorn, cookies, candy, cakes, chocolates, lollipops, gum, brownies, honey buns, apple sauce, powdered juice (tang), soda, soup, top ramen noodles, crackers, wheat thins, spam, sardines, octopus, tuna and chicken packets.

D is for Dentist

Do you have to make an appointment to see the dentist?
The dentist who works inside the prison is very similar to your dentist. When a prisoner is experiencing tooth pain or discomfort, they fill out a medical slip that is given to the dentist who schedules an appointment for the prisoner. The dentist works inside the prison to provide services for those prisoners who need dental assistance during their incarceration.

E is for Education

Are there teachers in prison?
Yes, there are many teachers in prison who work inside the correctional institution to teach those offenders who are interested in learning more. Teachers in prison have classes on science, math, language arts, reading, writing, anger management, Alcoholics Anonymous, Narcotics Anonymous, parenting classes and many others.

F is for Food

When are you allowed to eat in prison?
This is a good question. Prisoners are allowed to eat whenever they are hungry. The correctional institution provides inmates with food during scheduled breakfast, lunch and dinner times. When these meals are not being served prisoners can eat the snacks they have purchased from the prison commissary.

G is for Good Time

How does good time work?
This is a very good question. Good time works by allowing a prisoner who has followed the rules and regulations of their correctional institution to go home early. All prisoners are required to serve 80% of their sentence minus any earned good time. Prisoners who receive good time may become eligible for an early release, which will allow them to go home and serve the rest of their sentence under the supervision of a parole officer.

H is for Handcuffs

When will they take the handcuffs off of my parent?
I know this is an important question for you, because no child wants to see their parent in pain. When an officer takes off someone's handcuffs it is called being uncuffed. Individuals are uncuffed when they reach their next stop which is typically jail or the nearest police headquarters holding facility.

I is for Inmate

Why do they call my mom/dad an inmate?
Thank you for asking that question. Many people want to know the answer to that question. Your mom or dad is referred to as an inmate because it's a name given to all individuals who have been sentenced to serve time in prison. Prisoners all over the world have been called inmates. The term inmate can be used in any type of institution.

J is for Jobs

What kind of jobs do they have in prison?
There are many jobs in prison, similar to the jobs that you find individuals working within your own community. The type of work available in each prison varies depending on the availability of resources and security at that particular institution. Prisoners work inside and outside of their correctional facilities. Examples of jobs available to prisoners are: cooks, carpenters, janitors, barbers, hair stylists, legal aid assistants, clothing makers, license plate makers, electricians, engineers, landscapers, car mechanics, telemarketing, and maintenance workers.

K is for Keys

Why do correctional officers carry so many keys?
Correctional officers carry many keys because everything in the prison is kept closed by lock and key. All doors in the prison are locked shut to keep individuals from entering rooms without permission. When doors in the prison need to be unlocked, correctional officers use their keys to open them.

L is for Library

Do you get a library card in prison to check out books?
This is a great question. Prisoners do not have prison library cards, instead they use their inmate numbers to check out books that they would like to take back to their cells. Prisoners are usually able to check out up to 5 books at a time. Books must be returned to the library within 2 weeks.

M is for Mail

Can I send mommy/daddy mail to the prison?
Absolutely. You are able to send mail to your parent in prison whenever you wish. You can send as many letters as you wish to your incarcerated parent and/or family member. The letters can also be as long or as short as you'd like. To send a letter to your parent you will need an envelope, stamp, your parent's inmate number, and the full address of the correctional facility they are sentenced to.

For guidance on what to write about, visit www.projectironkids.com for information on Dr. Muhammad's workbook on letter writing for children of the incarcerated. This workbook provides activities that support healthy parent-child interaction during incarceration.

N is for Nurse

What happens if my parent gets sick in prison?
If your mom or dad gets sick while in prison, they go to see the prison nurse. The nurses give sick prisoners checkups and advice on how to get better. Nurses give shots to inmates who need them and perform annual checkups to make sure that they are in their best health.

O is for Officer

Who works in the prison to watch the inmates?
Correctional officers work inside the prison and watch over prisoners to make sure that they are following all the prison rules and regulations. If a prisoner breaks a rule, correctional officers will write them up and disciplinary action may be taken.

P is for Phone

Can I call the prison?
This is a very popular question among children of incarcerated parents. Many children desire to maintain contact with their parents and often wonder if they can just pick up the phone and call the prison to speak to their parent. Unfortunately, family members are not able to call the prison. Prisoners who have phone access can make collect calls home to their families and/or children.

Q is for Quiet Time

Where do you sleep in prison?
Inmates sleep in their cells during the time that they live in prison. Inmates have a bed, blankets and a pillow that they sleep on. Just like you sleep in your bed at night, prisoners also sleep inside a room in their bed.

R is for Radio

Can you listen to music in prison?
Yes, you can listen to music in the prison. In fact, prisoners can purchase a radio from the commissary. Prisoners can listen to music in their cells and outside in the yard.

S is for Schedule

What is your day like in prison?
Prisoners have very busy days while incarcerated. The day begins with waking up very early, followed by work. After work, inmates are served lunch and then must return to work in the early evening. After work inmates have the option to go outside in the yard. After yard time, dinner is served and followed by free time. After free time, inmates are locked into their cells and prepare to go to sleep for the night.

T is for Television

Where do you watch television?
Prisoners watch television with groups of other prisoners on their tier. Some of them have their own individual televisions in their cells. Individual televisions can be purchased through commissary.

U is for Uniforms

What do you wear in prison?
Every prisoner is required by law to wear a uniform. Uniforms are worn to distinguish inmates from other individuals working in the prison.

V is for Visit

Can you get a visit anytime you want?
Prisoners are not allowed to receive a visit at any time. In fact, each prison adheres to a strict visiting schedule that is made public on the Department of Corrections website for visitors to view. Correctional institutions allow visitors to come into the institution during the week and on weekends.

W is for Warden

Does the Warden live in the prison?
This is a good question. The warden does not live in the prison. Prisoners are the only individuals who live inside the prison. The warden usually lives on the same grounds as the prison in a very big house. The warden must always live close to the correctional facility because they may have to be at the facility in a short notice to deal with an emergency.

X is for X-ray

What happens if you fall and hurt yourself?
If prisoners get hurt while they are in prison they will go to see a doctor who will give them an x-ray to make sure that they did not break anything.

Y is for Yard

Can you play sports in the prison?
Yes, prisoners are allowed to play sports. During yard time many inmates play a variety of sports, such as basketball, soccer, wall ball, and kick ball. They can also lift weights, jump rope, and play chess, checkers and cards.

Z is for Zoo

Why does a cell look like cages at the zoo?
Cells have iron bars to keep inmates locked inside their room similar to the iron bars that keep animals locked inside their cage at the zoo.

Notes

Notes

About The Authors

Muntaquim Muhammad is an international philanthropist who has spent his life working to promote the welfare of impoverished children from Newark, New Jersey to Guguletu, South Africa. Currently, Muntaquim works as Road Manager to actor Michael K. Williams, known as Omar on HBO's *The Wire* and Chalky White on *Boardwalk Empire*. Throughout Mr. Muhammad's lifetime, he has aided children in Canada, Puerto Rico, Mexico, Prague, Cape Town, and Dubai. Most recently, Muntaquim is working alongside his wife Dr. Bahiyyah Muhammad with Freedom Productions to create a documentary film about children of incarcerated parents.

Dr. Bahiyyah Muhammad is an assistant professor of criminology at Howard University in Washington, DC. Bahiyyah has interviewed more than 500 children of the incarcerated and presented her research findings throughout the nation. Dr. Muhammad's ethnographic dissertation titled *"Exploring the Silence Among Children of Prisoners"* was groundbreaking in that it provided a well-rounded picture of the experiences of children in their own words.

Most recently, Mrs. Muhammad is working as Principle Investigator on a research project titled *"Far From The Tree: Resilient Children of Incarcerated Parents"*. This project highlights the remarkable experiences among children and young adults who have managed to succeed in light of parental incarceration. This study depicts real-world examples of children Dr. Muhammad defines as being *Iron Kids*.

Mr. and Mrs. Muhammad's next book *"100 Questions Children of Incarcerated Parents Ask"* will be published Spring 2014.

About Project Iron Kids

Established in 2013, Project Iron Kids is an initiative to increase the number of books for children of the incarcerated. Through literacy and education, we can help children understand the experience of having a mother and/or father in prison or jail, show children with parents in prison that they are not alone, and provide resources for caretakers to use to create opportunities to openly discuss the child's feelings and help them cope with their parents' absence.

For more information on Project Iron Kids and upcoming books aimed at children of incarcerated parents, visit www.projectironkids.com and subscribe to the mailing list for news and updates on the initiative.

Made in the USA
Middletown, DE
20 June 2019